EQUIZ
Newcomer

British Library Cataloguing in Publication Data
A catalogue record for this book is available from the British Library
ISBN 0.85131.652.2.
Published in Great Britain in 1996 by
J. A. Allen and Company Limited,
1 Lower Grosvenor Place,
Buckingham Palace Road,
London, SW1W OEL.

Typeset in Great Britain by Textype Typesetters, Cambridge.
Printed in Great Britain by Hillman Printers (Frome) Ltd, Somerset.

EQUIZ
Newcomer

VANESSA BRITTON

J. A. Allen
London

PART 1

Horse knowledge

Handling horses

1 Finish the sentence.

The horse is very much a creature of _____

a) habit   **b)** intelligence   **c)** arrogance

2 The horse appreciates a precise stable routine.
true ☐   false ☐

3 What are the 'golden rules' to bear in mind when handling a horse? Cross out the wrong words to make the sentences correct.

a) Speak *loudly/quietly*.

b) Avoid *sudden/slow* movements.

c) Handle *gently/harshly* but *cautiously/firmly*.

4 Which shows the correct way to tie a quick-release knot?

A ☐   **B** ☐   **C** ☐

5 Fill in the missing words from the list below (some words may be used more than once or not at all).

To control a horse when tying up or leading, a _____ is used. To put one on, first undo the buckle on the _____. Stand on the horse's _____ side and place a _____ around his neck, so that you have hold of him. Slip the _____ up over the horse's muzzle and place the _____ behind the horse's ears, so that it rests on his _____. Fasten the _____ until the _____ fits snugly.

cheekpiece	**lead rope**
bridle	**headpiece**
headcollar	**noseband**
right (off)	**poll**
left (near)	**brow-band**

6 What do the following sentences describe?

a) This is usually made of leather or synthetic materials and has a detachable rope.

_____

b) This is usually made of webbing or rope and is an all-in-one design.

_____

7 Yes or no?

a) Having tied a quick-release knot, should you push the loose end of the rope back through the loop to secure it?
yes ☐   no ☐

b) Should you use a piece of breakable string between the lead rope securing the horse and the tie ring?   yes ☐   no ☐

c) Is it acceptable to tie a horse to a haynet?   yes ☐   no ☐

d) Is it safe to tie a horse to a wooden gate?   yes ☐   no ☐

8 Name three things that are wrong with this picture.

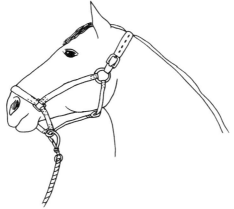

a) _____

b) _____

c) _____

9 What are the missing words?

When c_____ a horse in the f_____ first place the l_____ r_____ around his n_____ so that he cannot escape.

10 Should you speak to the horse as you approach him?

a) No, he will run off. ☐

b) Yes, he will be reassured. ☐

c) No, he will be startled. ☐

11 What subject is being discussed?

A horse should be accustomed to being _____ from both sides. If you were _____ a strange horse you would _____ it from the near side. Most horses are _____ in a headcollar but some may need to be _____ in a bridle. _____ a horse correctly is one of the most important aspects of horse management.

12 Which is the correct way to lead a lazy horse?

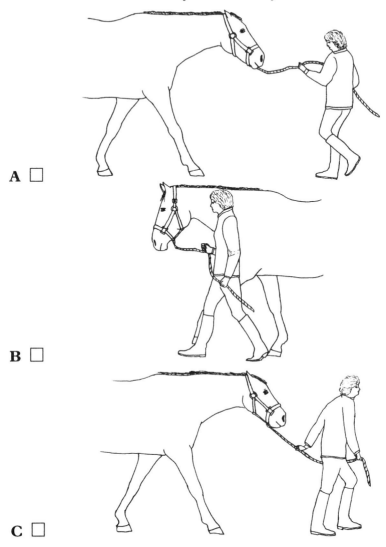

A ☐

B ☐

C ☐

13 When should a horse wear a bridle when being led?

_____

14 Make this sentence correct.

You _would/would not_ pass the reins over the horse's head when leading him in a bridle.

15 Which sentences are correct?

a) Do place your fingers through the D ring of the headcollar to hold the horse firmly.

b) Do not wrap the lead rope around your hand.

c) Do hold the cheekpiece of the headcollar if your horse plays up.

d) Do not stand in front of the horse and pull him if he won't move.

e) Do wrap the lead rope around your hand to help to hold the horse if he is strong.

f) Do wear gloves when leading in hand.

a ☐   b ☐   c ☐   d ☐   e ☐   f ☐

16 Which is the correct way to turn a horse?

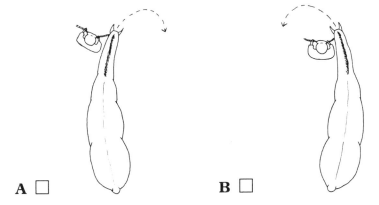

A ☐   **B** ☐

17 Finish the sentence.

If you stare at your horse in the face,

> **i)** he will probably refuse to move.
>
> **ii)** he will probably walk on obediently.
>
> **iii)** he will probably run away.

9

18 When trotting a horse up in hand you should allow the rope to be slack enough to enable him to carry his head naturally.
true ☐   false ☐

19 When standing a horse up in hand, should you stand in front of him and facing him?

a) No, as he will try to bite you.   ☐

b) Yes, this will enable you to keep his attention and keep him under control.   ☐

c) No, he will trample you.   ☐

20 From where should you approach the horse?

a) Head on.   ☐

b) The rear.   ☐

c) The front but slightly to the side.   ☐

d) The rear but slightly to the side.   ☐

Grooming

21 Join up the sentences.

a)	A horse should	**i)**	have his feet picked out first when grooming.
b)	A horse should not	**ii)**	be tied up when grooming.
c)	A horse should	**iii)**	be brushed with a body brush if living out in winter.
d)	A horse should not	**iv)**	have his tail combed with a mane comb.

22 Approximately how long should it take you to groom a horse fully?

a) 10 to 20 minutes. ☐

b) 30 to 60 minutes. ☐

c) One to two hours. ☐

23 Make the sentences correct by crossing out the wrong words.

Grooming is most effective when the horse is *warm/cold,* so it is best carried out *after/before* exercise. This is because the pores are *open/closed* and the body scurf is on top of the *skin/coat.*

24 Name these four items of a grooming kit:

A _____   **B** _____

C _____   **D** _____

25 Match up the sentences.

a) Quartering is

b) Strapping is

c) A full groom is

d) Setting fair is

i) a light brush-over in the evenings.

ii) the entire grooming procedure.

iii) a form of grooming massage.

iv) the removal of stable stains and a tidy up before exercise.

26 Fill in the missing grooming items from the list below.

First clear out the hooves using a _____. Then use a _____ brush to remove mud and heavy dirt. Next use a _____ brush to remove dust and scurf from the coat and clean this with a _____ comb. Use separate _____ to clean the eyes and nose and dock and finally polish over with a _____ _____

stable rubber	**body**
water	**sponges**
hoof pick	**curry**
dandy	**mane**
sweat scraper	**hoof oil**

27 Some horses are ticklish when being groomed and may bite through annoyance. What should you do to the horse before attempting to groom, to prevent yourself from being bitten?

_____

28 Which is the correct position for you to be in when picking out a hoof?

A ☐

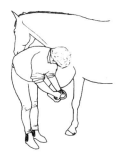

B ☐

29 What is the purpose of tying a cotton reel to a hoof pick?

_____

30 What is the missing word?

Apart from cleaning the horse, grooming also serves to stimulate the horse's c_____.

The horse's health

31 Put the following in order of priority when considering the horse's health:

	High	**Medium**	**Low**
• access to fresh water			
• sufficient grooming			
• the company of other horses			
• bathing			
• sufficient regular exercise			
• rugging up if cold			
• clipping out			
• regular feeding			
• access to safe grazing			

32 This stance is typical of a pony (less frequently of a horse) suffering from a common illness. This condition is often seen in overweight ponies grazing on lush grass – what do you think it might be?

L_____

33 If a horse is lame he is likely to rest his injured leg.

true ☐   false ☐

34 If a horse has an infectious disease what should be done with him?

a) He should be turned out in the paddock. ☐

b) He should be put in an isolation box. ☐

c) He should be bathed with warm soapy water. ☐

35 Match up the sentences.

a) A bruised wound is caused by   **i)** a kick, blow or a fall.

b) A puncture wound is caused by   **ii)** rubbing by dirty or ill-fitting tack.

c) A gall is caused by   **iii)** a nail or sharp object penetrating the skin.

36 Which is which?

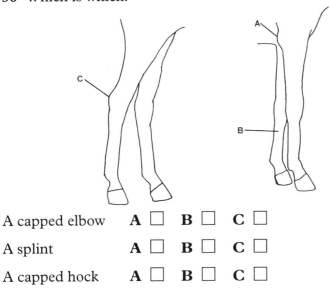

A capped elbow	**A** ☐ **B** ☐ **C** ☐	
A splint	**A** ☐ **B** ☐ **C** ☐	
A capped hock	**A** ☐ **B** ☐ **C** ☐	

37 What is being discussed?

This is a particularly common condition in winter, caused by wet, muddy conditions. The horse's legs, and possibly under his stomach, become encrusted with scabs which are very sore. The condition is more widespread in different parts of the country.
M_____ f_____

38 What is the term used for self-inflicted wounds on the inside of the fetlock joints?

a) Brushing. ☐

b) Cracked heels. ☐

c) Overreaches. ☐

39 You are picking a horse's feet out one day when you suddenly notice a strong and offensive smell. On further investigation, you find the frog has become spongy and there is a black discharge. What do you suspect is wrong with the horse? He has T_____

40 Which shows the average normal temperature range of a healthy horse at rest.   **A** ☐   **B** ☐   **C** ☐

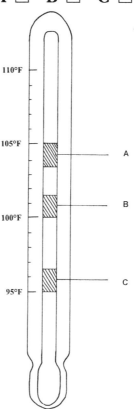

41 What is a windgall?

a) a chapped area, caused by wind blowing on a wet place   ☐

b) a wound caused by rubbing tack   ☐

c) a swelling just above the fetlock joint, which is often a warning of strain   ☐

42 If a horse had an infection or was in pain, would you expect him to have a raised temperature?   yes ☐   no ☐

43 A horse cannot vomit.   true ☐   false ☐

44 Which circled area shows where a horse's pulse is normally taken? **A** ☐ **B** ☐ **C** ☐

45 How do you test a horse for dehydration?

a) You offer him water to see if he will drink thirstily. ☐

b) You pinch his skin to see if it springs back into place or not. ☐

c) You check to see if he has a nasal discharge. ☐

Tack and turnout

46 From what material is tack traditionally made?

47 You can only use a snaffle bit with a snaffle bridle?
true ☐ false ☐

17

48 What components are missing from this snaffle bridle?

_____

_____

_____

49 Match up the sentences.

a) The two cheekpieces   **i)** hold/s the headpiece forward, behind the horse's ears.

b) The headpiece   **ii)** support/s the bit in the mouth.

c) The browband   **iii)** hold/s the cheekpieces in place.

50 What is being described?

A _____ is a complex system using two bits, a bridoon and a curb. In competent hands, a _____ offers precise control, but if used incorrectly it can cause much confusion and pain.

51 Select the correct measurements from those supplied below.

a) You should be able to place the width of _____ between the throatlash and the horse's jaw.

b) A cavesson noseband should allow the width of _____ between it and the horse's jaw.

c) You should be able to slide _____ comfortably under the browband.

two fingers   **your hand**   **one finger**

52 Which one of these bits has a nutcracker action?

A ☐

B ☐

C ☐

53 Join up the sentences.

a) A mullen mouthpiece

b) A single-jointed mouthpiece

c) A straight-bar mouthpiece

i) produces a nutcracker action.

ii) is slightly curved.

iii) has no curve.

54 What is being discussed? A _____ employs only one mouthpiece and is often used as an alternative to a double bridle. Two reins can be used, or only one when combined with bit roundings.

55 A bit fitted too low in the horse's mouth will allow the horse's tongue to come over the bit.   true ☐   false ☐

19

56 Which shows the correct measurement for determining a bit's size? **A** ☐ **B** ☐ **C** ☐

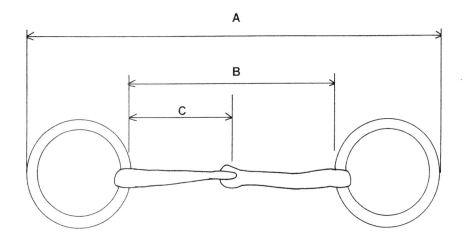

57 What is a hackamore?

a) A type of bit. ☐

b) A type of trekking saddle. ☐

c) A type of bitless bridle. ☐

58 Fill in the missing word. A headcollar designed for a foal is called a _____.

59 Cross out the wrong word in each case to leave the sentences correct.

a) The safety catch on stirrup bars should always be *up/down*.

b) If buying a new British saddle you should look for BSI number *BS6635/BS3656*.

c) When saddle-soaping tack, always wet the *sponge/soap* not the *sponge/soap*.

60 What should the measurements be between footwear and stirrup iron on either side of the foot?

The stable-kept horse

61 What minimum size of stable should a 15.2 hh horse occupy?

a) 2.4 x 3 m (8 x 10 ft). ☐

b) 3 x 3 m (10 x 10 ft). ☐

c) 3.6 x 3.6 m (12 x 12 ft). ☐

62 You are looking after a horse for your friend while she is away on a two-month holiday. She has told you that you must not use straw for his bedding as he coughs. You find that you cannot get a supply of his usual wood chippings, so do you choose sawdust or shredded paper as an alternative?
sawdust ☐   shredded paper ☐

63 Why?

---

64 Is this a good window design for a stable?

a) Yes, it has protective bars and the window opens inwards and upwards which prevents draughts. ☐

b) No, it has bars which are spaced too close together and the window should not open. ☐

c) No, it should not have bars and the window should open outwards and upwards. ☐

65 Make the sentence correct.
Hygienic/warm conditions are particularly important for horses because *germs/colds* and *illness/infection* thrive in *freezing/dirty* conditions.

66 What is meant by 'deep litter?'

_____

_____

67 Put the following in order of priority for the stable-kept horse:

	High	**Medium**	**Low**
• regular routine			
• large feeds			
• constant supply of hay			

- regular feeds

- fresh water

- rugs for warmth

- company of other horses

- adequate grooming

- access to grazing each day

- music playing

- exercise

- soft bedding

- ventilation

- being mucked out

68 This horse is 'cast', which means he has rolled over too close to the wall and cannot get up. What three things could you do to prevent this from happening again?

1 _____

2 _____

3 _____

69 Horses can sleep standing up.   true ☐   false ☐

70 Which of these sentences is correct when the horse is in the stable?

a) You should never tie a horse up when mucking out his stable.

b) If using a wheelbarrow to muck out, always have the handles pointing into the stable.

c) If the horse is nervous, always leave the door open while mucking out.

71 If the horse stands with his head over the door, rocking his head and neck from side to side and stepping from one foot to the other, what is he said to be doing? W_____.

72 Why should bales of hay or straw be stacked in this way?

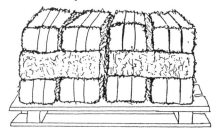

a) Because it makes it easier to get one off the stack.

b) Because it allows air to circulate and prevents them from heating up.

c) Because it prevents mice from nesting in them.

73 From which points would you measure to find a horse's rug size?

a) from the centre of the chest to the furthest point of the quarters. ☐

b) from the wither to the dock. ☐

c) from the wither to the lowest point of the horse's tummy. ☐

74 Join up the sentences:

a) A New Zealand   **i)**   is worn in the stable at night.

b) A day rug   **ii)**   is made of woollen material.

c) A night rug   **iii)** is worn while out in the field.

d) An anti-sweat rug   **iv)** is made of cotton mesh.

75 Make the sentence correct.
The *safest/worst* place for a water bucket in the stable is at *floor/waist* level. One at *waist/floor* level will be liable to have droppings and food dropped in it by the horse.

76 Which shows the correct way to tie up a haynet?

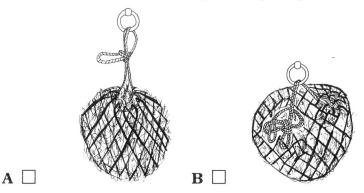

A ☐   **B** ☐

Feeding

77 What does a 'balanced diet' mean?

a) That each scoop of feed given weighs the same. ☐

b) That the roughage offered weighs the same as the concentrates. ☐

c) That the diet contains all the horse's nutrient requirements. ☐

78 All natural foodstuffs contain six basic components. Can you name three of them?

1 _____ 2 _____ 3 _____

79 Fill in the missing words.

The horse should eat _____ of his _____ _____ in food, per
_____. This should be divided between _____ and concent-
rated feeds, depending on how much _____ he is doing.

work	**height**
rest	**day**
2.5%	**week**
3.5%	**bulk**
6.2%	**water**
total	**bodyweight**

80 Which diagram represents the correct proportions of concentrates to bulk for a horse in light work? **A** ☐ **B** ☐

A   B

81 If you feed your horse at 7 o'clock in the morning, what is the earliest time you could ride him?

a) 7.30 am.   ☐

b) 8.00 am.   ☐

c) 9.00 am.   ☐

82 Why is fibre a most important ingredient of a horse's diet?

_____

_____

83 The horse has a stomach equal to the size of a dustbin, which is why he can consume large amounts at once.   true ☐   false ☐

84 Which arrow points to the horse's stomach?
A ☐   **B** ☐   **C** ☐

85 Cross out the wrong words to make the sentence correct.
The horse should *never/always* have access to a *fresh/warm* supply of water before feeding.

Horse behaviour

86 If a horse was presented with a frightening or possibly painful situation, what would he do?

a) Run away.   ☐

b) Stand up and fight.   ☐

c) Nothing.   ☐

87 Which of the following is correct?

a) Horses are individuals and must be treated as such. ☐

b) Punishment and reward are the fairest methods of dealing with horses. ☐

c) Horses have the same kind of intellect as humans. ☐

d) Solitary horses cannot suffer from insecurity or loneliness. ☐

88 If you noticed your horse looking like this in the field, would you be unduly worried?

a) No, I would think he was resting. ☐

b) Yes, I would bring him in and examine him straightaway. ☐

c) Yes, I would come back later to check that he had not got any worse. ☐

89 Horses are herd animals, which means they will generally only thrive when in the company of others.   true ☐   false ☐

90 Fill in the missing words to complete the sentences.

The horse's main defence is his _____, combined with quick _____. He has a _____ speed of 22 kmph (35 mph) which is about equal to that of his natural _____ so his chances of escape are _____.

teeth	sprinting
hindlegs	predators
speed	friends
reactions	50/50
hearing	25/75
idling	100

91 How should you approach a horse?

a) Go up and pat him on the head. ☐

b) Stand to one side, talk to him, let him sniff you before stroking his neck. ☐

c) Walk backwards towards him without talking. ☐

92 If a horse looked like this as you approached him, would you be happy to touch him?

Physical characteristics

93 What is being discussed?

It contains approximately 205 bones. It includes the axial skeleton, which comprises the skull, ribs, spinal column and breastbone, and the appendicular skeleton, made up of the pelvis and limbs.

94 What is conformation?

a) It is the make and shape of the horse. ☐

b) It is the muscles of the horse. ☐

c) It is the systems of the horse. ☐

95 Join up the sentences.

a) A half-bred is:

b) An Anglo-Arab is:

c) A warm-blood is:

i) a cross between an Arab and a Thoroughbred.

ii) of European origin, but not a pure breed.

iii) a cross between a Thoroughbred and any other breed.

96 Fill in the labels for the parts of the horse.

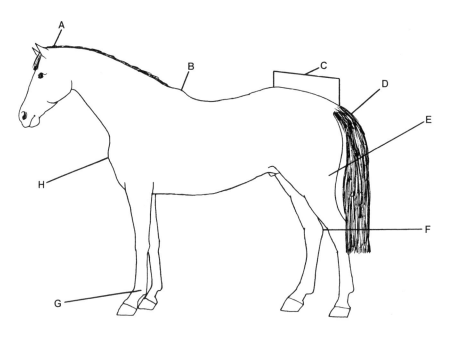

97 Fill in the missing words for colours of horses.

a) A _____ has large, random patches of white and any other colour except black.

b) A _____ has white hairs throughout his coat, which may be of various colours.

c) A _____ has a brown coat with black points.

98 How do you determine a horse's age?

a) By counting the rings around his hoof. ☐

b) By a blood test. ☐

c) By examining his teeth. ☐

99 You are asked to take a look at a horse's feet. You find they have flat soles, are fairly large and very sloping with low heels. Do you decide the feet are: strong ☐   weak ☐

100 Some of these labels have got mixed up. Can you sort them out?

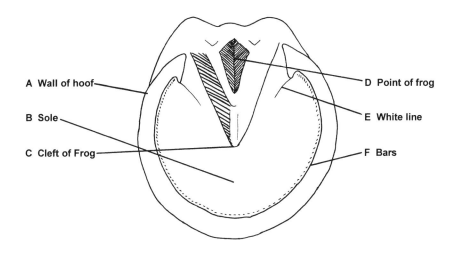

A Wall of hoof

B Sole

C Cleft of Frog

D Point of frog

E White line

F Bars

PART 2
Riding

Tacking up

101 Cross out the wrong words to make the sentences correct.

Hold the saddle and place it on the *withers/loins,* more *backward/forward* than usual. Slide it *forwards/backwards* with the direction of the *hair/skin* until it comes to a natural resting place. In its correct position, the *cantle/pommel* will be above the rear of the *quarters/withers.*

102 From which side is the girth normally fastened?
near side ☐   off side ☐

103 A girth is sufficiently tight when:

a) You cannot put your hand between it and the horse's side. ☐

b) You can just slip the flat of your hand between it and the horse. ☐

c) You can put a fist between it and the horse's side. ☐

104 What is wrong with the illustration on page 33? Can you name three faults?

1 _____

2 _____

3 _____

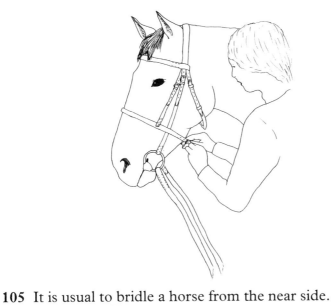

105 It is usual to bridle a horse from the near side.

true ☐   false ☐

106 Immediately before bridling, what two things must you ensure are *undone*?

1 _____

2 _____

107 When the horse is good to bridle, it is usual simply to pull the headpiece up the face with the right hand and slip the bit into the mouth with the left, but what can you do if the horse tries to lift his head.

a) You can use a stronger bit.　　　　　　☐

b) You can slip your right arm under the horse's jaw and hold both cheekpieces on the front of his face while guiding the bit in.
　　　　　　☐

c) You can put on a headcollar and tie the horse up very short so that he cannot lift up his head.　　　☐

33

108 Would you say this girth was:

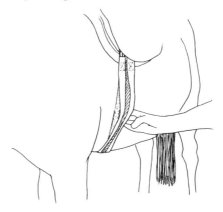

a) Too tight ☐

b) Too loose ☐

c) About right ☐

109 What is being discussed? Having put on the bridle you should do up the _____ first for security. Check to see that you can get the width of your hand between it and the horse's face.

110 Join up the sentences.

a) The headpiece   **i)** encourages the horse to open his mouth to take the bit.

b) The thumb   **ii)** supports the cheekpieces and bit.

c) The browband   **iii)** prevents the headpiece from slipping backwards.

Mounting

111 How can you judge (approximately) the length of stirrup leather you are going to need before mounting?

a) By measuring your inside leg. ☐

b) By holding your knuckles on the stirrup bar and adjusting the length until the iron reaches into your armpit. ☐

c) By using a third of your height measurement. ☐

112 Which girl is standing in the correct position for mounting?

A ☐ **B** ☐

C ☐

113 There are four possible ways of mounting, can you name three of them?

1 _____   2 _____

3 _____

114 Fill in the missing words from the list below.

When mounting from the near side, put your _____ foot in the stirrup and push your toe down. Pivot around on the _____ leg so that you are looking over the saddle and put your _____ hand on the _____ or far- or near-side _____, not the _____. Put your left hand on the _____ or _____ and spring up from the _____ leg. Lift your _____ leg over the quarters and lower yourself gently into the saddle.

saddle	**pommel**
flaps	**cantle**
left	**withers**
right	**neck**

115 You must never mount from the off side.   true ☐ or false ☐

116 Is this the correct way to shorten a stirrup?

a) No, she should have her foot out of the stirrup.   ☐

b) No, she should be using both hands.   ☐

c) Yes, this is the safest method.   ☐

117 Having mounted, what should you check?

a) That the girth is tight. ☐

b) That the saddle fits correctly. ☐

c) That the horse is not lame. ☐

118 What is being discussed?

The rider stands squarely, facing the saddle, with his or her left lower leg bent up backwards from the knee. An assistant stands to the left of the rider, takes hold of the rider's left knee in the left hand and supports the rider's ankle with the right hand. On an agreed command, usually one, two, three, the rider springs up, aided by the assistant and lowers him/herself gently into the saddle.

---

119 Is this sentence correct?

If your leathers are too short you will appear to be 'perched' in the saddle and look as though you are sitting too far back.
yes ☐   no ☐

120 Which is the correct way to hold the reins?

A ☐   **B** ☐

Dismounting

121 To dismount correctly should you:

a) Take both feet out of the stirrups and swing your right leg over the horse's quarters, sliding gently to the ground? ☐

b) Keep your left foot in the stirrup and swing your right leg over the horse's quarters sliding gently to the ground. ☐

c) Take both feet out of the stirrups and swing your right leg over the horse's withers, sliding gently to the ground. ☐

122 Having dismounted, what should you always do with the stirrups and, if not untacking immediately, with the girth?

_____

_____

123 You should always throw your whip to the ground before dismounting: true ☐   false ☐

124 Comment upon the way in which this rider is dismounting.

_____

_____

125 Having dismounted, should you:

a) Take the reins over the horse's head in order to lead him back to the stable. ☐

b) Clip a lead rope on to the bit in order to lead him back to the stable. ☐

c) Just take hold of the left rein and lead him back to the stable. ☐

A correct position

126 Why is there such a thing as a correct position?

_____

_____

127 Cross out the wrong words to make the sentences correct.

You should sit in the *central/forward, deepest/shallowest* part of the saddle. Your *seat/leg* bones should take equal weight, with your *knee/spine* pointing directly to the horse's *spine/loins* and your seat muscles should be *relaxed/taut*.

128 Would you say that this rider has a good riding position?
yes ☐ no ☐

129 Why?

_____

_____

130 Join up the sentences:

a) The heel should be   **i)**   relaxed against the saddle.

b) The knee should be   **ii)** lower than the toe.

c) The calf should be   **iii)** resting close to the horse's side.

131 What is being discussed?

When you take hold of the reins, you will feel some weight in your hands and will have a link with the horse's mouth. Ideally, this 'feel' should be constant throughout all the gaits. This is known as

_____

132 It is desirable to have a straight line from the elbow down the reins to the bit as is seen here. Why?

a) Because this allows your forearm to become (in effect) an extension of the reins, which ensures a sensitive contact through the subtle movements of your elbows and shoulders. ☐

b) Because you can then ride with any length of rein. ☐

c) So that you do not have to move your arms if the horse puts his head up or down. ☐

133 Join up the sentences:

a) At walk

i) your trunk should remain upright and your hips and back should be supple, absorbing the movement of the horse.

b) At rising trot

ii) your trunk should be inclined slightly forward from the hips so that you remain in balance with the horse's movements.

c) At sitting trot

iii) your trunk position does not alter except that it moves slightly at the hips and waist, in line with the natural movements of the horse's head and neck.

134 Where should you look when riding?

a) Straight between the horse's ears. ☐

b) To the left or right depending on which way you are going. ☐

c) Down at the line of the track upon which you are riding. ☐

135 What is meant by an 'armchair' position?

_____

_____

Natural aids

136 How many natural aids can you see here?

137 What is the purpose of the aids?

a) They help us to convey our wishes to the horse. ☐

b) They force the horse to do as he is told. ☐

c) They prevent the horse from evading the bit. ☐

138 Which statements are true?

a) Each leg and hand should be able to work independently but in conjunction with each other.

b) The left leg and hand, and the right leg and hand, should work together.

c) The actions of both hands should be identical at all times.

d) The actions of both legs should be identical at all times.

139 If you constantly tap at your horse with your legs, you will reduce the sensitivity of his sides. true ☐ false ☐

140 When turning the horse, you have one leg on the girth to create impulsion and give the horse something to bend around, and one leg behind the girth to stop the hindquarters from falling out. Armed with this information, take a look at the diagrams and say which is the rider's *inside* leg and which the *outside* leg.

A inside ☐ outside ☐ **B** inside ☐ outside ☐

141 To ask the horse to move forwards would you:

a) Apply pressure from each leg alternately. ☐

b) Use the whip just behind the leg. ☐

c) Apply pressure from both legs at the same time. ☐

142 The horse can understand actual words and so can learn to walk on or trot by voice alone, whoever is issuing the commands. true ☐ false ☐

143 In very general terms, explain what your inside hand is responsible for and what your outside hand is responsible for.

_____

_____

144 Which diagram represents the basic seat position at halt and which the driving seat position for moving the horse forwards?

A _____ **B** _____

145 To ask the horse to go forward into trot from walk would you?

a) Place one leg on the girth and one leg behind the girth, squeezing alternately. ☐

b) Place both legs on the girth and squeeze together. ☐

c) Place one leg behind the girth and one leg on the girth, squeezing together. ☐

Artificial aids

146 What is the purpose of artificial aids?

a) They are used to punish the horse. ☐

b) They are used to reinforce the natural aids. ☐

c) They are used to make the horse go slower. ☐

147 Apart from whips and spurs, what other items of equipment are technically classed as artificial aids?

_____

_____

148 Which is the correct way to wear spurs?

A ☐   **B** ☐

149 Where should the schooling whip be used?

a) Just behind the lower leg. ☐

b) On the horse's neck. ☐

c) On the horse's rump. ☐

150 If you have gritted your teeth while using a stick, you have probably lost your temper and acted out of anger.
true ☐   false ☐

The horse's gaits

151 Join up the sentences.

a) The walk is
b) The trot is
c) The canter is

i) a two-beat gait.

ii) a four-beat gait.

iii) a three-beat gait with a period of suspension when all four feet are off the ground.

152 Which of these horses is

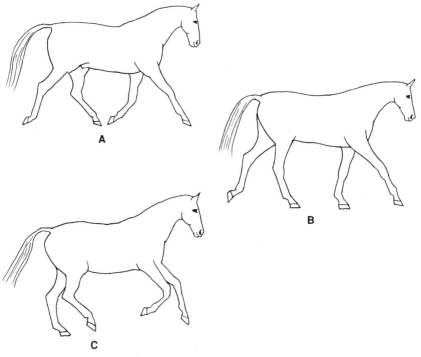

A

B

C

a) Walking   A ☐   B ☐   C ☐
b) Trotting   A ☐   B ☐   C ☐
c) Cantering   A ☐   B ☐   C ☐

153 What gait is being discussed?

The horse uses its legs in diagonal pairs. The near fore and off hind work together, as do the near hind and off fore.

---

154 In the walk, the horse always has at least two feet on the ground. Can you put the sequence of foot falls in order?
near fore ☐   near hind ☐   off fore ☐   off hind ☐

155 To what gait does the term leading leg refer? _____

School figures and exercises

156 Which figure represents the riding of a serpentine in the school?   **A** ☐   **B** ☐   **C** ☐

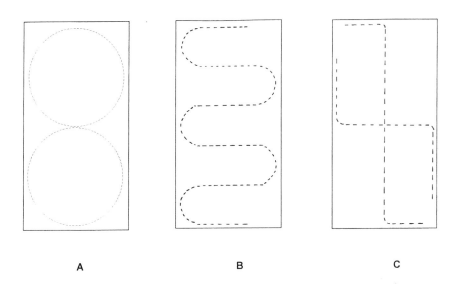

A   B   C

157 Before performing exercises, it is usual to remove the stirrups from the saddle or cross them over the withers. What should you do first to ensure that the leather lies flat?

158 Fill in the missing words.

R_____ t_____ w_____ s_____is quite strenuous. It helps to strengthen the thigh muscles and inner knee and will increase versatility and strength rather than riding skills but should only be practised for a short time at first to avoid strain.

159 Join up the sentences.

a) Ankle rolling   **i)** will loosen the knees and help to achieve a deeper seat.

b) Trunk twisting   **ii)** will loosen the waist and lower back.

c) Leg swinging   **iii)** will loosen the joint and help the leg to lie flat against the horse's side.

160 If you rode across the school like this, what would you be doing?

_____

_____

161 In the scissors exercise you end up facing the horse's tail.
true ☐   false ☐

162 To help to create suppleness at the start of a horse and rider's training, should you use:

a) Large circles   ☐

b) Small circles ☐

c) Only straight lines ☐

163 Fill in the missing words.

To be accurate on a _____, the horse must travel around its _____ with his body _____, from his _____ through to his _____, to match precisely the _____ of the _____.

circle	**head**
curve	**circumference**
bent	**tail**

164 Cross out the wrong words so that the sentence explains what is happening here.

Scissors/round the world is a popular exercise which improves *fitness/suppleness, co-ordination/mental agility* and *balance/strength*.

165 What is meant by 'going large'?

a) Riding all the way round the outside track of the school. ☐

b) Doubling the size of the circle you are currently riding. ☐

c) Asking the horse to perform longer strides down the length of the school. ☐

Lungeing

166 How large is the average radius for lungeing a rider?

a) 10 metres ☐

b) 20 metres ☐

c) 30 metres ☐

167 The whole purpose of lungeing is for the rider to be able to distinguish between the horse's gaits and paces.
true ☐   false ☐

168 Lungeing without stirrups is most beneficial for achieving a good position. Would you say this was basically a good position?

a) Yes, the rider is sitting up straight and in balance. ☐

b) No, the rider is slouched and her heel is not down. ☐

c) No, but only because the rider is looking downwards. ☐

169 Initially, all riders should be encouraged to maintain their balance by holding on to the front of the saddle. Is this true?

a) Yes, it allows the rider to experience riding over the horse's centre of gravity. ☐

b) No, it restricts the rider from developing a good seat. ☐

c) No, it prevents the rider from using any of the natural aids. ☐

170 Fill in the gaps.

Most work on the lunge is done in _____ because it has an easy _____ _____ rhythm.

Safety wear

171 It is not acceptable to ride with loose, long hair. Why and what could you do about it?

_____

172 When riding, you should always wear an approved riding hat which, in the UK, will bear a British Standard Institute (BSI) number. Which of these hats are safe and which are not?

A safe ☐ not safe ☐ **C** safe ☐ not safe ☐

B safe ☐ not safe ☐ **D** safe ☐ not safe ☐

173 Why?

_____

_____

174 What is the best type of footwear for riding?

a) A long boot with a suitable heel. ☐

b) Wellington boots with a small heel. ☐

c) Trainers with no heel. ☐

175 Name two reasons why it is sensible to ride in gloves.

1 _____

2 _____

The Highway Code

176 What is the signal being given here and to whom is it being directed?

_____

_____

177 Does the Department of Transport Highway Code apply to riders? yes ☐ no ☐

178 Are you allowed to ride or lead a horse on a public footpath or pavement by the side of the road?

a) Yes, at any time. ☐

b) Yes, but only after lighting-up time. ☐

c) You are only allowed to lead a horse on a pavement. ☐

d) Not at any time. ☐

179 Two broken white lines across the mouth of a junction mean that you must stop. true ☐ false ☐

180 Rule 219 of the Highway Code states that horse riders must carry lights if riding at night. Here we can see a suitable stirrup model, but what colour should be showing to the front and what colour to the rear?

a) Red to the front; white to the rear. ☐

b) White to the front; orange to the rear. ☐

c) Red to the front; orange to the rear. ☐

d) White to the front; red to the rear. ☐

Road safety

181 What minimum insurance should any rider hold?

a) Third party legal liability ☐

b) First party legal liability ☐

c) Horse party legal liability ☐

d) Personal accident ☐

182 Complete the sentence.

When horses are on the road:

a) They must give way to all other traffic. ☐

b) They have the right of way. ☐

c) They have the same rights and responsibilities as other road users. ☐

183 Can a rider be breathalysed for being drunk in charge of a horse on the public highway?   yes ☐   no ☐

184 Here we can see a rider clearly informing the traffic to the front and rear that she intends to turn right – but is she doing so in the safest way?

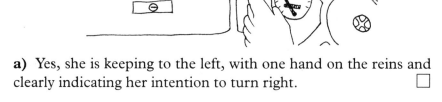

a) Yes, she is keeping to the left, with one hand on the reins and clearly indicating her intention to turn right. ☐

b) No, she should have pulled over to the right next to the white line. ☐

c) No, she should have dismounted and waited on the pavement until all traffic had cleared. ☐

185 If a car were travelling towards you at 31 kmph (50 mph), how far away would it have to be in order to avoid you if your horse shied into its line?

a) 53 m (175 ft) ☐ **b)** 47 m (155 ft) ☐ **c)** 59 m (195 ft) ☐

186 Make the sentence correct.

When leading a horse on foot on a road, you should keep to the *left/right* of the road with *yourself/the horse* between *the horse/yourself* and the traffic.

187 What two things should you remember to do if you have to go out riding in the snow?

1 _____

2 _____

188 Here we can see a rider overtaking a parked car – but is she doing so safely?

a) No, she should have dismounted. ☐

b) No, she should have pulled over to the right-hand side of the road to give the car more clearance. ☐

c) Yes, she is in full control. ☐

189 What three things in particular should the rider in this picture be looking out for?

1 _____

2 _____

3 _____

190 Could you be considered liable if your horse caused harm or damage to other people or their property while on the public highway?   yes ☐   no ☐

Emergency action

191 Be Safe Be Seen – what does this message convey?

a) That you should ride towards the flow of traffic so that they can see you. ☐

b) That you should only ride in large numbers so that it is easy to see your group. ☐

c) That you should wear light-reflective or fluorescent clothing and lights, depending on the weather conditions. ☐

192 If one of your riding companions fell off and knocked themselves out, you would put them in this position. What is this position called?

193 Why is it important to put an unconscious person in this position?

a) Because it will prevent them from choking on inhaled vomit or blood, or the tongue from blocking the airway. ☐

b) Because it will make them more comfortable. ☐

c) Because it will prevent them from breaking their spine. ☐

194 If you come across a fallen rider who is unconscious, should you remove their hat? yes ☐ no ☐

195 How would you control the bleeding of a wounded rider?

a) Place a clean handkerchief over the wound and apply pressure. ☐

b) You should not do anything as it will stop naturally. ☐

c) Get them to hold the wounded part up high. ☐

Jumping

196 What is this type of jump called?

197 Why is it such a useful piece of equipment?

_____

_____

198 When a horse lands, one foreleg meets the ground fractionally before the other and so, momentarily, takes the full weight of the horse's body. true ☐ false ☐

199 What is the correct word to describe the shape a horse makes over a fence when jumping in good style?

a) Bascule ☐

b) Culebask ☐

c) Rounded ☐

200 This is known as the jumping position. Which of the following statements are true regarding this position?

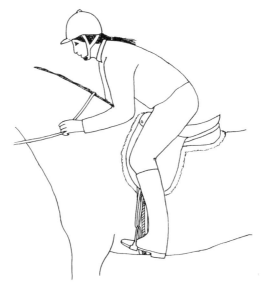

a) You need to shorten your stirrups in order to achieve it.

b) It closes the angles at the hip, knee and ankle joints.

c) Because the horse's centre of balance moves further forward the faster it goes, the rider has to equal this by getting further forward too.

d) There is still a straight line between elbow, hand, rein and bit, although the hand can move forwards in the direction of the bit.

Answers

Part 1 Horse knowledge

Handling horses

1a) Habit – the horse learns and lives by repetition.

2 True, horses are content if they are fed or turned out at the same time each day, but can become fretful if their routine alters.

3a) Speak *quietly*.
b) Avoid *sudden* movements.
c) Handle *gently* but *firmly*.

4c) A knot tied in this way can quickly be released by pulling on the end of the rope.

5 To control a horse when tying up or leading a *headcollar* is used. To put one on, first undo the buckle on the *cheekpiece*. Stand on the horse's *left (near)* side and place a *lead rope* around his neck, so that you have hold of him. Slip the *noseband* up over the horse's muzzle and place the *headpiece* behind the horse's ears, so that it rests on his *poll* . Fasten the *cheekpiece* until the *headcollar* fits snugly.

6a) A headcollar; **b)** a halter.

7a) No, this would prevent it from being pulled undone quickly in an emergency.
b) Yes, as this will release the horse in the event of an emergency if the quick-release knot cannot be pulled.
c) No, should he pull it down, he could get his feet caught in it, which could cause a nasty accident.
d) No, were he to pull back he could snap the plank and run off with it trailing between his legs, causing injuries to himself or an accident involving someone else.

8a) The headcollar is too big.

b) The lead rope should be clipped so that the opening faces the horse's neck, not his lip.

c) The headpiece is done up on its last hole.

9 When *catching* a horse in the *field* first place the *lead rope* around his *neck* so that he cannot escape.

10b) Yes, he will be reassured.

11 Leading a horse.

12 B, it is no good pulling a horse who will not walk, as he will only pull back all the more. You must drive from behind.

13 When he is on the public highway.

14 You *would* pass the reins over the horse's head when leading him in a bridle, unless he is wearing a martingale.

15b) d) and **f)** are correct.

16 Away from you, so **A** is correct.

17 If you stare at your horse in the face, he will probably refuse to move.

18 True.

19b) Yes, this will enable you to keep his attention and keep him under control.

20 From the front but slightly to the side, so **C** is correct

Grooming

21 a) + i); **b)** + iii); **c)** + ii); **d)** + iv).

22b) 30–60 minutes.

23 Grooming is most effective when the horse is *warm* so it is best carried out *after* exercise. This is because the pores are *open* and the body scurf is on top of the *coat*.

24 A hoof picks **B** metal curry comb **C** body brush **D** dandy brush

25 a) + iv); **b)** + iii); **c)** + ii); **d)** + i).

26 First clear out the hooves using a *hoof pick*. Then use a *dandy* brush to remove mud and heavy dirt. Next use a *body* brush to remove dust and scurf from the coat and clean this with a *curry* comb. Use separate *sponges* to clean the eyes and nose and dock and finally polish over with a *stable rubber*.

27 Tie the horse up short.

28 B is correct. Never kneel, as in diagram **A**, as you would not be able to escape quickly if the horse moved suddenly.

29 It enables it to be quickly located if dropped in the horse's bedding.

30 Apart from cleaning the horse, grooming also serves to stimulate the horse's *circulation*.

The horse's health

31	**High**	**Medium**	**Low**
	• access to fresh water	• the company of other horses	• sufficient grooming
	• regular feeding	• sufficient regular exercise	
	• access to safe grazing	• rugging up if cold	• clipping out
			• bathing

32 Laminitis.

33 True.

34b) He should be put in an isolation box.

35 a) + i); **b)** + iii); **c)** + ii).

36 A a capped elbow; **B** a splint; **C** a capped hock

37 Mud fever.

38a) Brushing.

39 Thrush.

40 B.

41c) A swelling just above the fetlock joint, which is often a warning of strain.

42 Yes.

43 True.

44 B, where the facial artery passes under the jaw.

45b) You pinch his skin to see if it springs back into place or not.

Tack and turnout

46 Leather.

47 False, you could use any single bit with a snaffle bridle, for example a Pelham.

48 The *reins*, *browband* and *throatlash* are missing.

49 a) + ii); **b)** + iii); **c)** + i).

50 A double bridle.

51a) You should be able to place the width of *your hand* between the throatlash and the horse's jaw.
b) A cavesson noseband should allow the width of *two fingers* between it and the horse's jaw.
c) You should be able to slide *one finger* comfortably under the browband.

52 A.

53 a) + ii); **b)** + i); **c)** + iii).

54 A Pelham bit.

55 True.

56 B.

57c) A type of bitless bridle.

58 A headcollar designed for a foal is called a *foalslip*.

59a) The safety catch on stirrup bars should always be *down*.
b) If buying a new British saddle you should look for BSI number *BS6635*.
c) When saddle-soaping tack, always wet the *soap* not the *sponge*.

60 1–1.5 cm (about ½ in) on either side of the foot.

The stable-kept horse

61c) Any smaller and he may get cast.

62 Shredded paper.

63 Sawdust is not a dust-free bedding, whereas paper bedding is.

64a) Yes, it has protective bars and the window opens inwards and upwards, which prevents draughts.

65 Hygienic conditions are particularly important for horses because germs and infection thrive in dirty conditions.

66 Deep litter is a bedding system whereby only the droppings are removed from the top of the bed. The bed continually has clean bedding laid over the top to keep it dry and clean. It only works well if used in a fairly large stable.

67 High	Medium	Low
• regular routine	• rugs for warmth	• music playing
• constant supply of hay	• adequate grooming	• soft bedding
• regular feeds	• access to grazing each day	
• fresh water	• being mucked out	
• company of other horses		
• exercise		
• ventilation		

68 1 Bank up the sides of the bed. **2** Place the horse in a larger stable.
3 Use an anti-cast roller.

69 True, they have a 'stay' mechanism which enables them to do so.

70 None of them is true; in fact, you should do exactly the opposite of all of them.

71 He is *weaving*, which is a stable vice.

72b) Because it allows air to circulate and prevents them from heating up.

73a) From the centre of the chest to the furthest point of the quarters.

74 a) + iii); **b)** + ii); **c)** + i); **d)** + iv).

75 The *safest* place for a water bucket in the stable is at *waist* level. One at *floor* level will be liable to have dung and food dropped in it by the horse.

76 B is correct. **A** could be pulled tight, which would allow the net to hang low, perhaps resulting in the horse getting his foot caught in it.

Feeding

77c) That the diet contains all the horse's nutrient requirements.

78 You could have three of: proteins, carbohydrates, fats and oils, vitamins and minerals.

79 The horse should eat *2.5%* of his *total bodyweight* in food, per *day*. This should be divided between *bulk* and concentrated feeds, depending on how much *work* he is doing.

80 A is correct. Rarely does the amount of concentrates exceed that of bulk, especially for a horse in light work.

81b) 8.00 am. You should allow an hour before exercise, otherwise a full stomach may interfere with the horse's breathing.

82 Fibre provides roughage which helps to keep the horse's digestive system healthy.

83 False. The horse's stomach is relatively small for the size of his body, so he can consume feeds only 'little and often'.

84 A.

85 The horse should *always* have access to a *fresh* supply of water before feeding.

Horse behaviour

86a) Run away – the horse's main defence is flight.

87 a) and **b)** are correct; **c)** and **d)** are incorrect.

88b) Yes, I would bring him in and examine him straightaway.

89 This statement is true.

90 The horse's main defence is his *speed*, combined with quick *reactions*. He has a *sprinting* speed of 22 kmph (35mph) which is about equal to that of his natural *predators* so his chances of escape are *50/50*.

91b) Stand to one side, talk to him, let him sniff you before stroking his neck.

92 No, he looks extremely angry and would most likely try to bite you.

Physical characteristics

93 The horse's skeleton.

94a) It is the make and shape of the horse.

95 a) + iii); **b)** + i); **c)** + ii).

96

A	=	poll
B	=	withers
C	=	croup
D	=	dock
E	=	thigh
F	=	hock
G	=	fetlock joint
H	=	point of shoulder

97a) A *skewbald* has large random patches of white and any other colour except black.

b) A *roan* has white hairs throughout his coat, which may be of various colours.

c) A *bay* has a brown coat with black points.

98c) By examining his teeth.

99 Feet such as these are generally weak.

100

A	=	wall of hoof
B	=	sole
C	=	point of frog
D	=	cleft of frog
E	=	bars
F	=	white line

Part 2 Riding

Tacking up

101 Hold the saddle and place it on the *wither*, more *forward* than usual. Slide it *backwards* with the direction of the *hair* until it comes to a natural resting place. In its correct position, the *pommel* will be above the rear of the *withers*.

102 The girth is normally, but not exclusively, fastened from the near side.

103b) You can just slip the flat of your hand between it and the horse.

104 The bit is too low; the browband is too low; the noseband is too high; the noseband is being fastened around the cheekpieces; the reins are hanging down.

105 True, as most of the buckles are done up on this side.

106 1 *the noseband;* **2** *the throatlash.*

107b) You can slip your right arm under the horse's jaw and hold both cheekpieces on the front of his face while guiding the bit in.

108b) It is too loose, so the saddle will slip if the rider tries to mount.

109 *Throatlash.*

110 a) + ii); **b)** + i); **c)** + iii).

Mounting

111b) By holding your knuckles on the stirrup bar and adjusting the length until the iron reaches into your armpit.

112 B, once their left feet are in the stirrups, she is the only one who could still control the horse adequately.

113 From the ground; leg up; vaulting and mounting block.

114 When mounting from the near side put your *left* foot in the stirrup and push your toe down. Pivot around on the *right* leg so that you are looking over the saddle and put your *right* hand on the *pommel* or far- or near-side *saddle flap*, not the *cantle*. Put your left hand on the *withers* or *neck* and spring up from the *left* leg. Lift your *right* leg over the quarters and lower yourself gently into the saddle.

115 False, you may need to do so in a number of cases, so it is sensible to practise from time to time.

116c) Yes, this is the safest method.

117a) That the girth is tight.

118 Having a leg-up.

119 Yes.

120 A, this will enable you to do so sensitively.

Dismounting

121a) Take both feet out of the stirrups and swing your right leg over the horse's quarters, sliding gently to the ground.

122 Run up the stirrups and loosen the girth.

123 False, this may make the horse jump, so causing a possible accident.

124 He is using the stirrup which is not to be recommended unless you have some form of disability and you also have an assistant holding the horse.

125a) Take the reins over the horse's head in order to lead him back to the stable (unless he is wearing a martingale).

A correct position

126 Sitting in the correct position will enable you to sit comfortably, remain in balance and apply the aids correctly.

127 You should sit in the *central, deepest* part of the saddle. Your *seat* bones should take equal weight, with your *spine* pointing directly to the horse's *spine* and your seat muscles should be *relaxed*.

128 Yes.

129 This vertical line is deemed to denote a good riding position. She is also sitting symmetrically in the saddle and so is not hindering the horse's balance in any way.

130 **a)** + ii); **b)** + i); **c)** + iii).

131 This is known as *the contact*.

132a) Because this allows your forearm to become (in effect) an extension of the reins which ensures a sensitive contact through the subtle movements of your elbows and shoulders.

133 Join up the sentences: **a)** + iii); **b)** + ii); **c)** + i).

134a) Straight between the horse's ears.

135 An 'armchair' position is where the rider leans backwards against the cantle, with the lower leg pushed right forwards as if slouching in an armchair.

Natural aids

136 Four: the seat, voice, legs and hands.

137a) They help us to convey our wishes to the horse.

138a) True.
b) False.
c) False.
d) False.

139 True, such actions also encourage him to 'switch off'.

140 A outside; **B** inside.

141c) Apply pressure from both legs at the same time.

142 False, the horse understands what is required from the *tone* of the voice, so the same word said in different tones will provoke a different response.

143 The inside hand gives subtle aids which control the direction. The outside hand maintains a steady, but firm, contact which controls the speed.

144 A Basic position; **B** driving seat.

145b) Place both legs on the girth and squeeze together.

Artificial aids

146b) They are used to reinforce the natural aids.

147 Martingales and forms of dropped noseband.

148 B is correct.

149a) Just behind the lower leg.

150 True, any punishment should be given swiftly but must be calculated and justified.

The horse's gaits

151 a) + ii); **b)** + i); **c)** + iii).

152 **A** is trotting; **B** is walking; **C** is cantering.

153 The trot.

154 **1** near hind; **2** near fore; **3** off hind; **4** off fore.

155 Canter. It refers to the leg which the horse leads with, which should be the inside foreleg.

School figures and exercises

156 B.

157 You should slide the buckle down so that it does not rub against your thigh.

158 *Rising trot without stirrups.*

159 a) + iii); **b)** + ii); **c)** + i).

160 You would be changing the rein across the diagonal in order to go around the school the other way.

161 True. You then reverse the exercise to face forwards again.

162a) Large circles, as neither horse nor novice rider can cope with the demands of riding small circles.

163 To be accurate on a *circle*, the horse must travel around its *circumference* with his body *bent*, from his *head* through to his *tail*, to match precisely the *curve* of the *circle*.

164 *Round the world* is a popular exercise which improves *suppleness, co-ordination* and *balance.*

165a) Riding all the way round the outside track of the school.

69

Lungeing

166a) 10 m (this would be on a 20-m circle).

167 False. The purpose of lunge lessons is to help the rider adopt the correct position in the saddle and to enable them to learn to sit still in relation to the horse's movement without having to worry about controlling him as well.

168b) No, the rider is slouched and her heel is not down.

169a) Yes, it allows the rider to experience riding over the horse's centre of gravity.

170 Most work on the lunge is done in *trot* because it has an easy *two-time* rhythm.

Safety wear

171 Long hair can easily blow into the face and obstruct vision, or it may get caught on low branches. Either tie it up or use a hairnet.

172 **A** and **D** are safe.

173 **B** is not safe because it has only a two-point harness; **C** is not safe because it appears to have had a blow and the harness is splitting.

174a) A long boot with a suitable heel.

175 They will prevent chafing from rubber or hard reins. They will prevent leather reins from slipping through your hands in wet weather. They will keep your hands warm, which, in cold weather, will ensure that you can keep hold of the reins properly.

The Highway Code

176 The signal is stop and it is being directed to road users from both in front and behind.

177 Yes, it applies to any road user.

178d) Not at any time.

179 False. A solid white line means stop. You must slow down and give way to vehicles with right of way.

180d) White to the front; red to the rear.

Road safety

181a) Third party legal liability. All riders and owners are strongly recommended to have this, and the BHS and Pony Club extend such cover to their members.

182c) When horses are on the road they have the same rights and responsibilities as other road users.

183 No.

184a) Yes, she is keeping to the left, with one hand on the reins and clearly indicating her intention to turn right.

185a) 53 m (175 ft).

186 When leading a horse on foot on a road you should keep to the *left* of the road with *yourself* between *the horse* and the traffic.

187 Smear thick grease on the soles and frogs of your horse's feet. Carry a hoof pick while out riding.

188c) Yes, she is in full control.

189 1 Oncoming traffic; **2** anybody opening the car door; **3** anything trying to overtake from behind.

190 Yes.

Emergency action

191c) That you wear light-reflective or fluorescent clothing and lights depending on the weather conditions.

192 The recovery position.

193a) Because it will prevent them from choking on inhaled vomit or blood, or the tongue from blocking the airway.

194 No, as you do not know if they have damaged their neck. Wait for the emergency services.

195a) Place a clean handkerchief over the wound and apply pressure.

Jumping

196 A cavaletto (plural cavaletti).

197 Because its height can be altered simply by turning it. It can be used in grids, in trotting work, within courses and so on. However, cavaletti must never be stacked up on top of each other.

198 True.

199a) Bascule.

200 They are all true.